# EGYPTIAN ART

SPRING ART BOOKS

# Egyptian Art

BY J. R. HARRIS

SPRING BOOKS · LONDON

# ACKNOWLEDGMENTS

The works in this volume are reproduced by kind permission of the following collections and galleries to which they belong:

The Visitors of the Ashmolean Museum, Oxford (Plates 30, 31, 46); Staatliche Museen zu Berlin (Figures 9, 11, 23, Plate 16); Staatliche Museen der Stiftung Preussischer Kulturbesitz, Berlin-Dahlem (Figure 1, Plates 26, 32, 33); Museum of Fine Arts, Boston (Plate 6); The Trustees of the British Museum, London (Figures 6, 16, Plates 23, 24, 38, 45, 47, 52); Brooklyn Museum, New York (Plate 12); Egyptian Museum, Cairo (Figures 3, 5, 7, 10, 12, 13, 15, 17, 18, Plates 1, 3, 4, 7, 9, 11, 14, 19, 20, 27, 34, 35, 36, 37, 39, 43, 44, 50, 51, 53); Oriental Institute of the University of Chicago (Plates 15, 55); Egypt Exploration Society, London (Figure 20); The Syndics of the Fitzwilliam Museum, Cambridge (Plates 17, 18); Fundação Calouste Gulbenkian, Oeiras (Figure 14); Musée du Louvre, Paris (Plates 5, 10, 29, 40, 42, 49, 54); The Metropolitan Museum of Art, New York (Figures 8, 19, 21); Museo Egizio, Turin (Figures 22, 24, Plate 2); University College, London (Plates 13, 28). Figures 19, 21 are reproduced from *The Tomb of Rekh-mi-rē at Thebes* by N. de Garis Davies. © Metropolitan Museum of Art, New York, 1943.

The following photographs were supplied by: Brompton Studio, London (Plate 15); Werner Forman, Prague (Figures 5, 7, 13, 15, Plates 1, 3, 4, 9, 11, 14, 16, 19, 20, 22b, 27, 37, 39, 43 44, 50, 51, 53); Raymond Fortt, London: Spink and Son Ltd. (Figure 1); Griffith Institute, Oxford (Figures 3, 17); Hirmer Verlag, Munich (Plate 22a); Jacqueline Hyde, Paris (Plates 5 10, 29, 40, 42, 49, 54); F. L. Kenett, © George Rainbird Ltd. (Plate 36); Arpag Mekhitarian, Brussels (Plate 35); Stearns, Cambridge (Plates 17, 18); UNI-DIA Verlag, Stuttgart (Plates 21a, 21b, 25, 34); Roger Wood, London (Figures 4, 10, 12, 18, Plates 7, 8, 41, 48).

*Published by*
SPRING BOOKS

Drury House • Russell Street • London WC2
© Paul Hamlyn Ltd. 1966
*Printed in Czechoslovakia by Svoboda, Prague*
T 1628

# CONTENTS

# CHRONOLOGICAL TABLE

All dates before 664 BC are approximate.

BC

| | |
|---|---|
| 5000—3000 | Badarian and Predynastic Periods |
| 3000 | Union of Upper and Lower Egypt (plus or minus 150 years) |
| 3000—2700 | Protodynastic Period (first and second dynasties) |
| 2700—2200 | Old Kingdom (third to sixth dynasties) |
| 2200—2050 | First Intermediate Period (seventh to mid-eleventh dynasties) |
| 2050—1785 | Middle Kingdom (later eleventh and twelfth dynasties) |
| 1785—1575 | Second Intermediate Period (thirteenth to seventeenth dynasties) |
| 1575—1075 | New Kingdom (eighteenth to twentieth dynasties) including the Amarna Period (1375—1355) |
| 1075— 332 | Late Period (twenty-first to thirtieth dynasties) including the Saite period (twenty-sixth dynasty 664—525) |
| 332— 30 | Greek Period |
| BC30—AD395 | Roman Period |

# INTRODUCTION

Until the beginning of the nineteenth century and the sudden enthusiasm for Egyptian antiquities that followed Napoleon's expedition and the discovery of the Rosetta Stone, the art of pharaonic Egypt was virtually unknown except as interpreted by Imperial Rome and through the fanciful imitations of the Renaissance. Since then it has become increasingly familiar, both in itself and by the adaptation of its forms and decorative motifs, but although its influence extends from the ubiquitous churchyard obelisk to the costume jewellery of today Egyptian art remains, nevertheless, extraneous to European culture and, unlike the art of classical antiquity, has no essential place in its aesthetic heritage. For this reason, and because the principles and underlying purpose of Egyptian artistic representation are quite alien to Western ideas, a conscious detachment from the 'ideal' standards of fifth-century Greek sculpture or the painting of the Italian and Dutch masters is necessary in approaching their Egyptian counterparts. Such detachment is indeed less difficult now than it was in 1821-2 when London flocked to see Belzoni's 'curious remains of antiquity' in the Egyptian Hall in Piccadilly, or when Mariette revealed the art of the Old Kingdom to an unsuspecting Parisian public at the great exhibition of 1867, for with the rise of the modern art movements and their deliberate rejection of traditional concepts the tyranny of 'photographic' representationalism has been broken, and much of the prejudice attached to art that is formalised or intellectual has been dissipated. But whereas the intellectual character of contemporary work is quite apparent, Egyptian art is curiously deceptive and, by reason of its antiquity, is apt to be regarded merely as underdeveloped or inept, and the true nature of its ideographic processes misunderstood. In fact, the manner of Egyptian representation, though admittedly unusual, is neither inadequate nor immature, but simply the outcome of a different approach to the problem of artistic communication, and cannot therefore be fully appreciated without some understanding of the basic attitudes and presumptions which lay behind it.

Emotive notions of art as springing from man's spiritual nature or as the inspirational expression of imaginative feeling are altogether meaningless in relation to ancient Egypt, and indeed to speak of Egyptian 'art' at all is in a sense to beg the question, for the Egyptians themselves had evolved no corresponding term, but referred indiscriminately to 'handicraft', writing the word with a sign depicting the borer used in hollowing out stone vases. To them the process of artistic representation was an essentially practical exercise conditioned by a fundamental faith in the magical nature of things and in magic itself as an elementary dynamic force which permeated all their thinking. They believed in fact that the artist or craftsman could through his work call into being both living creatures and material objects and effectively re-create activities and situations, and further that by so doing he might bridge the gulf of death and ensure the continuity of life in a recognisable form. From as early as the protodynastic period the verb *mesi* — to give birth — was also used with reference to artistic reproduction, while in the New Kingdom a common word for sculptor was *seankh*, the literal meaning of which is 'he who makes to live' (figures 1 and 2). A statue therefore, which might as it happened become a thing of beauty, was primarily destined to a more vital end, to secure by magical means the survival of the person represented — or in the case of a deity to provide a habitation for the divine presence — and a figure properly inscribed with the name and titles of an individual became thereby endowed with the nucleus of his personality, an incorruptible body underwriting his post-mortem existence. Similarly, a relief or painting was thought potent to revive the circumstances it represented; a scene depicting the owner of a tomb amid the varied pleasures of life on earth being adequate to promote these same diversions in the life beyond (plates 21, 22, 23 and 24), while one in which a religious observance was perpetuated would tacitly assure the gods of man's unfailing concern for their well-being (plates 31 and 48).

2  The sculptor Iuti at work

8

Since his creations were designed for eternity, the Egyptian craftsman tended as far as possible to work in enduring materials — though economic and other considerations would often dictate the use of less satisfactory substitutes — and this in itself played no small part in moulding the character of Egyptian art. Moreover, in order adequately to fulfil its magical purpose, any representation, whether in three dimensions or two, was required to be immediately and absolutely explicit and comprehensible, and in general therefore both sculptor and draughtsman sought to communicate a rational objective truth independent of time and space, and to show things in what were deemed to be their real and immutable forms, free from such purely visual effects and distortions as might constitute an obstacle to identification. Attributes of essential significance and even abstract characteristics were depicted symbolically (plates 19, 46 and 51) — importance, for example, being translated into size (figures 3 and 4 and plates 22 and 23) — and there was thus no incongruity in the realisation of wholly imaginary entities such as the hybrid deities and other venerable grotesques which peopled the world of Egyptian religious speculation (plates 45 and 51). Colour too was evidently regarded as intrinsic, though in the event it was often more or less conventionally expressed, and as a further means of conveying information and to define what was not otherwise apparent descriptive 'labels' and inscriptions were commonly added (plates 1, 5, 8, 13, 14, 41 and 45). In that anything thus explicitly reproduced was thought literally to be re-created, it became axiomatic that the choice of subject matter and the manner of its presentation should mirror the Egyptian view of things as they ought to be, and that the portrayal of the potentially harmful or disturbing should be avoided, to the extent even that noxious hieroglyphs were in some cases deliberately mutilated. Indeed, in Egyptian art, as in the philosophy of Voltaire's Dr Pangloss, all was for the best in the best of all possible worlds — given that this best of worlds was one in which Egypt remained the master and the *status quo* was timelessly preserved.

The predominance of straight lines and block forms in Egyptian art and architecture is often interpreted as the conscious expression of a rectilinear space concept in harmony with the natural contours of the Nile valley and the grandeur of its scenery, but while it can scarcely be denied that such forms were ultimately satisfying to the Egyptian mind, their evolution is largely attributable to technical developments The cubic character of Egyptian statuary, for example, was not determined by aesthetic considerations but was merely the inevitable consequence of the particular method evolved for working the hardest stones with only the most elementary tools, while the bold lines of pharaonic architecture, though again suggestive of a definite norm, were primarily the result of the conservative translation into stone of elements derived from more primitive constructions in less permanent materials. The curious illusion of geometry apparent in some representations, particularly of the human figure, is similarly incidental — the deliberate construction of significant spatial relationships being out of the question, if only because of the relative crudity of Egyptian mathematics. That these exist is simply because in executing the preparatory sketches on a wall, or on a block intended for a statue, the Egyptian draughtsman made use of a system of intersecting guide lines, such that any figure drafted in conformity with it will of necessity possess certain inherent geometric qualities.

The Egyptian approach to artistic creation being thus essentially practical, the modern concept of the artist as an individual creative personality was almost entirely lacking, at least until the New Kingdom. Like other craftsmen, the majority of sculptors and painters were paid artisans, rigidly trained, who worked as members of a team, faceless executants with no real opportunity for self expression, whose technical skill or versatility might incidentally secure for them a measure of personal recognition — as in the case of the 'overseer of craftsmen' Irtysen, of the eleventh dynasty, 'a craftsman excellent in his craft who rose to the top through what he knew'. And while the names of more than a few sculptors and others, some of considerable social standing, are known from their private monuments and from the inclusion of their figures in the tombs of their masters, it is but rarely that the craftsman responsible for a particular piece of work can certainly be identified. When credit is given it is usually to the patron, though in most cases he can scarcely have done more than commission a monument or authorise its general character, and even where evidence suggests that an individual artist may have exercised an overall control, the extent to which he was in fact involved in the actual execution cannot really be assessed. It is, on the other hand, apparent that in many instances, notably in the drafting of relatively minor elements in tomb reliefs and paintings, craftsmen now unhappily anonymous have shown considerable enterprise (figure 21 and plates 8, 21, 23 and 24), adding fresh details to already familiar compositions and occasionally, as in the tomb of Senbi at Meir, transforming whole scenes by new and adventurous treatment. In such circumstances it is tempting, as with some outstanding sculptures, to interpret the work as that of a master artist, but however great the influence exerted by a particular individual it seems probable that the finished product was generally the outcome of collective endeavour.

To what extent the Egyptian craftsman inclined to specialise it is difficult to gauge, but to judge from the scenes in which workshops are depicted it would appear that initially he may have been trained to work in a particular medium, the making of statues in wood and metal being thus the province of the carpenter and metalworker, while the stonemason was both sculptor and vase maker. It may be, too, that a mason accustomed to carving limestone or alabaster was not in general required to work the harder rocks which demanded greater skill, though there are indications that in some cases a single studio turned out sculptures in a variety of stones. Whatever the circumstances of their training, the master craftsmen were, however, more versatile, and it is clear that often they became adept in all branches of art, handling different materials with equal facility and turning alike to sculpture, draughtsmanship or handicraft. Thus Senwosret, the son of Irtysen, is described as 'overseer of works in every precious material from silver and gold to ivory and ebony', while architects such as Ineni and the deified sages Imhotep and Amenhotep son of Hapu, also called Huy, will surely have been skilled in all aspects of their work.

The ingrained conservatism of the Egyptian outlook and the limitations of the magico-religious approach tended inevitably to inhibit innovation, and with relatively few exceptions Egyptian art objects of whatever period are instantly recognisable as such. Through almost three millennia, down to the conquest of Alexander and even beyond, the individual style already apparent at the beginning of the first dynasty and crystallised during the protodynastic period survived with little radical alteration. But although in a sense Egyptian art remained thus static, the initial impression of absolute continuity and resistance to change is in fact misleading and clear lines of historical development may be distinguished. Changes in social and economic conditions, subtle yet fundamental shifts in intellectual attitudes and ever increasing influence from neighbouring lands had each their effect, marking with a definite character the art not only of the great ages of Egyptian civilisation, but even of the formative periods which preceded them.

In spite, however, of such extraneous pressures, the underlying principle of retooling for eternity, though gradually somewhat modified, persisted, and representational art continued to be essentially a vehicle for the perpetuation of human activity. To this extent the only substantial break in the continuity of Egyptian artistic tradition was that accompanying the religious 'revolution' of the Amarna period which substituted for the familiar deities of the pantheon the worship of the Aten, the power manifest in the sun's disk (plate 27). Rejection of the old gods, and more particularly of the accepted mythology of the after-life invited a reappraisal of the basic attitude to art, and the idealised expression of objective reality was consciously renounced in favour of the more immediate truth of subjective visual perception. Significant changes were made in the form of two-dimensional representation, though certain established usages were never abandoned, and statuary too was treated with greater freedom, as is clear from the surviving fragments of some composite sculptures and other unusual pieces (figures 10 and 13 and plates 28 and 29). But the new 'realism' was subject to its own conventions, the figures of the royal family in particular being often grotesquely distorted (figure 18 and plate 27), and this peculiar mannerism was only less extreme in products of the later years of Akhenaten's reign (plates 32 and 33). That the king himself was in some measure responsible for the new wave may be inferred from the statement of the sculptor Bak (figure 1) that he was 'an assistant whom his majesty himself taught', but the part played by the principal court artists should not be overlooked. Of necessity, the practical interpretation of any such royal instruction will have been largely dependent upon their ability to adjust to a fresh outlook, the apparently enhanced status of men like Bak and Iuti, Parennefer and Thutmose suggesting that collaboration was not without its reward.

The descriptive character of Egyptian art is most clearly apparent in two-dimensional representation, that is in painting and relief, which may reasonably be considered together in that the conventions applied to them and the initial stages in their execution were so essentially similar. To the Egyptians relief appears indeed to have been no more than a reinforced or durable species of drawing, and it was never therefore consciously three-dimensional in concept, the seemingly anomalous full-face figures in high relief such as those standing within niches (figure 1) plainly being conceived as statues attached to a dorsal slab.

The earliest incised figures and rudimentary reliefs, of predynastic date, are found on knife handles, combs and other objects of wood, bone and ivory and on ordinary slate palettes, the sudden emergence of a distinctively Egyptian style being marked by the elaborate sculpturing of the large ceremonial palettes and mace-heads of the period immediately preceding the first dynasty. By the beginning of the Old Kingdom the technique of carving low relief was already far advanced, as shown by the wooden panels of Hesirē (plate 1), and the quality of the work in many tombs of the fourth and fifth dynasties (plates 5 and 8) is in some respects unequalled by that of later periods. During the Middle Kingdom the tradition of finely modelled low relief was maintained (plate 14), but greater use was also made of sunk relief (*relief en creux*),

3 Tutankhamūn victorious over the
Nubians

5 The chief of Pwenet and his consort

4 Ramses III hunting wild cattle

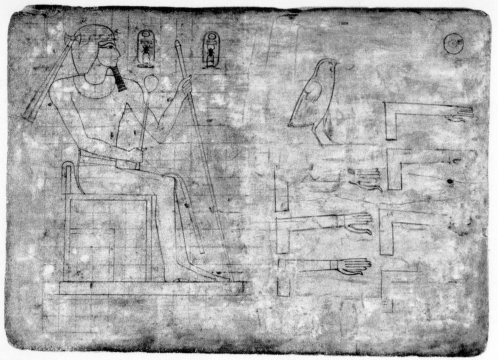

6 Drawing board with canonical master-drawing

7 Sculptor's trial piece

8 Unfinished decoration in a tomb

9 Unfinished relief

10 Unfinished head

11 Sculptor's trial study of a head

12 Unfinished statue

13 Unfinished statue

14 Head of a statue of Senwosret III

15 Statuette of the dwarf Seneb and his family

16 Block statue of Sennefer

17 Statue of the goddess Selket

18 Colossal statue of Akhenaten

not only on walls but on inscribed slabs (stelae) and sarcophagi, presumably because it weathered better and was more easily seen in a strong light (plate 13). Under the eighteenth dynasty and until the beginning of the nineteenth both forms were common, and some examples of low relief of this period are of particular delicacy (plates 25, 40, 41 and 42), but thereafter — save during the Saite period (twenty-sixth dynasty) — sunk relief was more usually employed, especially in the decoration of temple walls and the towers of pylon gateways (figure 4).

Apart from the painting on certain classes of predynastic pottery, the earliest surviving examples, of similar date, are some fragments of simple designs daubed on bits of plaster, leather and other materials, and portions of two more substantial compositions with human figures and boats, one on linen, the other on the wall of a tomb. Some royal funerary monuments of the first dynasty were also ornamented with panels of coloured patterning, but the oldest known representational paintings which are typically Egyptian are from two tombs of the third and early fourth dynasties respectively (plate 4). Not until the sixth dynasty did painting become more usual, beginning gradually to supersede relief in private tombs, no doubt for economic reasons, and from this same dynasty there is indirect evidence of easel work, though what may have been its purpose remains obscure. Painted decoration, often quite elaborate, was common on wooden coffins of the first intermediate period and of the Middle Kingdom, to which belong also a number of outstanding murals such as those in the tomb of Khnemhotpe at Beni Hasan (plate 15). It was, however, in the eighteenth and nineteenth dynasties that painting came into its own, its widespread use in the Theban necropolis (plates 21, 22, 23 and 24) being due largely to the condition of the limestone which was generally unsuitable for carving reliefs. During the New Kingdom and later, painting was also much employed in the illumination of papyrus 'books' (plate 45) and as a cheaper form of ornamentation on mummy cases, furniture and other wooden objects (figure 3), though from the end of the nineteenth dynasty there was a steady decline in quality.

The first preliminary to the execution of a relief or painting was the preparation of the ground, which varied according to the nature and quality of the surface on which the work was to be carried out. In the case of relief, for which ideally the coarsest materials were not employed, a careful smoothing of the face of the stone, or wooden panel, was often adequate, though a larger area such as a wall would usually require patching with gypsum plaster to make good fissures in the rock or mask the division between individual blocks. Occasionally, when the condition of the stone was unsuitable, a whole wall might be coated with a layer of plaster in which the relief was in fact carved, the refinement of this technique in certain tombs of the New Kingdom being such that the delicate modelling seems merely to underline the painted figures (plate 48). In the case of mural painting too, a good stone surface was often simply smoothed and patched where necessary, the paint then being applied directly, or over the thinnest wash of fine plaster. More frequently, however, and especially in the tombs at Thebes where the natural rock was poor, the wall was levelled with a thickish layer of mud plaster and finished with a thin coat of gypsum or whiting to take the paint, and a similar facing was also usual on walls of brick. Wood was as a rule surfaced with plaster before being painted, but this was not always the case, and much of the decoration on the early coffins was done on the timber itself.

Once the ground had been adequately prepared the intended composition was drafted, the degree of precision and detail depending largely upon the scale of the work and its importance. Thus in the laying out of a wall or other similar area the general disposition of the various elements had to be determined and the outlines of individual figures and objects sketched in, and although the drawing might sometimes be executed freehand, and with remarkable sureness (figures 7 and 8), more often it was done with the aid of guide lines, both vertical and horizontal. The use of these intersecting lines, which from the Middle Kingdom became systematised in the form of a squared grid, was not, however, a mere convenience, their essential function being to ensure that the human figures should be correctly proportioned in accordance with a fixed canon (figure 6). The guide lines were ruled or made with a string dipped in pigment, and the sketches themselves drawn either with a brush of fibrous wood or with a rush 'pen' such as was used by scribes. In most instances the initial drafts were in red, but when necessary the details were later corrected, usually in black and presumably by another hand, and the wall was then ready to be carved or painted (figure 8).

In cutting a relief the sculptor first chiselled round the corrected outlines of the separate elements, further emending the line from time to time as he felt inclined, and, in the case of low relief, reduced the level of the background so as to leave a series of flat shapes standing out (figure 9). The figures were then worked over and their forms modelled, and after the repair of minor defects the whole was finally painted and outlined, often over a thin wash of plaster. In some New Kingdom sunk reliefs in coarse sandstone, the figures were boldly carved in quite deep recesses and finished with a comparatively substantial plaster coating in which the interna details were largely worked. Quite frequently, the inscriptions and decorative

18

motifs accompanying either form of relief were merely incised (plates 27 and 40).

The painter, whether working to a corrected draft or colouring a relief, began by washing in the background, usually blue-grey, white or yellow, for which he seems to have used a stumpy brush of halfa grass or palm fibre. He then proceeded to paint the figures and objects, beginning as a rule with the flesh tints, and for this employed pieces of fibrous wood of different thicknesses bruised at one end to form coarse bristles. The final stage was the outlining and drawing of internal details which, like the initial sketch, was done with a narrow fibre brush or a scribe's 'pen', the subsequent application of a resinous varnish in a few Theban tombs of the eighteenth dynasty being quite exceptional (plate 21). What appears to have been a unique method of 'painting', intended to make the representations more permanent, is known from a tomb of the fourth dynasty, outlines sunk in the limestone being filled with pigment in solid masses.

Egyptian painting was never fresco, as it is frequently described, but a type of distemper or *gouache*. Water, alone or mixed with gum, was the vehicle, and the principal pigments were either naturally occurring minerals, finely ground, or artificial preparations from mineral substances. The basic colours of the Egyptian palette were six in number — red, yellow, blue, green, black and white — and the corresponding pigments most commonly used during the pharaonic period were red iron oxide or red ochre, yellow ochre or orpiment, powdered azurite or blue frit, powdered malachite, chrysocolla or green frit, carbon black and gypsum or whiting. There was, however, considerable variation in these 'primary' colours, the ochres for example running to nuances of brown, and intermediate shades were readily obtained by laying one pigment over another or by mixing. In the New Kingdom in particular the use of more subtle tints was not uncommon, and experiments were also made in creating the illusion of transparency (plates 21, 42 and 48) and, more rarely, with shading (figure 3 and plates 24 and 48). The Egyptian painter tended, nevertheless, to work in flat colours, interpreting natural hues according to certain established conventions, but sometimes his choice was altogether arbitrary, and simple decorative effects might also be achieved by unexpected combinations and contrasts. Where painting was purely ornamental the polychromy was frequently quite sophisticated, the rich design of many ceiling patterns reflecting an instinctive feeling for harmony of form and colour.

Although the broad content of a relief or painting was dictated by convention and the underlying requirements of magical belief, the actual format of any representation was largely governed by the need to decorate a given space. It was indeed the size and shape of the ground on which a composition was to be executed that determined its scale and influenced the layout of its principal elements, for rarely were parts of a surface left blank, except at the foot of a wall. The area thus presented, which might be further defined by a formal border (figure 3 and plates 35 and 42), was to the Egyptian draughtsman a space to be filled completely and at the same time a framework within which all the essentials of a situation had so to be contained that nothing implied extension of the action beyond its confines.

With relatively few exceptions, the subject matter of two-dimensional representations is typical rather than specific, events being portrayed in a quite general way with no distinctive details to identify the particular circumstances, which may, however, be indicated in accompanying inscriptions (figures 3 and 4 and plate 45). The scenes in a tomb are thus idealised pastiches, reiterating recurrent themes from life, while even historical events are apt to lose their real identity, the record of a victorious battle being at once a symbolic memorial of the fact and a magical perpetuation of Egyptian superiority (figure 3). Precise identification of locality is rare outside the ambitious tableaus of some Ramessid temple reliefs, such as those recording military campaigns, and when sketched in at all, scenic background is usually indicated more or less schematically, though often with a genuine feeling for nature (figure 4 and plates 22 and 23). Effects of distance and true perspective as we understand it were not recognised, and although experiments were made in the treatment of massed groups of figures, notably during the New Kingdom, all but the simplest compositions are as a rule divided into registers — horizontal strips each with a separate base line. When the division is spatial, as for example in banqueting scenes (plates 21 and 24), the lowest of these registers represents that which is nearest to the viewer, while within a register objects behind or inside others are generally shown above. Where it is temporal, the separate registers may depict a succession of events — as sowing, reaping and threshing — or stages in a single operation, a series of figures in the same register being sometimes used to illustrate continuous action, rather in the manner of a strip cartoon. In either case, however, the principle is essentially the same, namely to show events not as they may appear to the eye of the observer from a particular standpoint or at a given moment, but as they are known to be, with conscious rectification of appearances conditioned by space and time.

For similar reasons subjective sensations are also avoided in depicting individual figures and objects, the simpler ones being shown, like hieroglyphs, in their most characteristic aspect, generally profile or plan, while the more complex are built up artificially from typical views of their essential components, producing an almost diagrammatic summary of the thing as it really is. The most developed of these descriptive diagrams is that evolved for the representation of the ideal human figure (figure 6 and plate 1), a composite form in which profile, three-quarter and frontal views are so combined that when drafted according to the canon the constructed proportions of the body are coincident with those of nature. Thus the head is drawn in profile, but with the eye in what amounts to its frontal aspect, the shoulders are seen as from the front, the breast in profile, and the waist and hips in a three-quarter view with the navel visible, while both feet usually show the inside and the hands are often identical.

In view of the re-creative nature of Egyptian art, it was natural that the content of any composition and the manner in which separate elements were portrayed should in a measure reflect an ideal concept of the human condition. But while the main features of a relief or painting are as a rule somewhat stylised, the treatment of insignificant elements is often less conventional, a contrast particularly apparent in the case of human figures. Of these the larger and more important are always artificially constructed in the manner described, whereas minor figures, normally on a smaller scale, are quite often freely and experimentally drafted — and without reference to the canon (figure 8). By this same class distinction, true profile, though applied to

19 Stonemasons at work

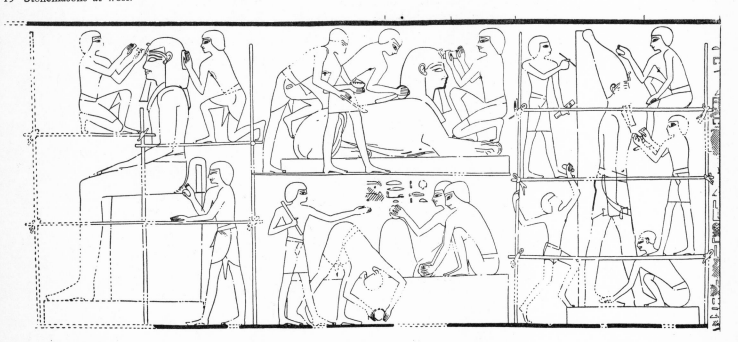

animals (plate 8) and to inanimate objects including, significantly, the majority of statues (figure 19), is in the case of people confined almost exclusively to aliens and servants, where it is not uncommon (figure 20 and plates 21 and 24). Full-face, back, and three-quarter views, which are in any case rare, are similarly restricted (figures 19 and 21 and plate 24). Though the principals are ever calm and dignified, much greater freedom of movement is permitted to lay figures, many of which are indeed no more than hieroglyphs for the actions they perform. Attempts, not always successful, are made to represent unusual poses and awkward bodily contortions (figures 3, 19, 21 and 22), and even emotion may be crudely expressed, as in the gestures of mourners in funeral processions. Nor do the nonentities invariably share the ageless well-being of their superiors; poverty, starvation, disease and old age are all from time to time depicted (figure 5), while total disorder and human misery are implicit in the tumbled heaps of dead and dying in battle scenes (figure 3). But in all this there is no inconsistency, for the condition of inferiors was of small importance in the world of the Egyptian draughtsman.

Many of the basic conventions were, however, modified during the Amarna period, when two-dimensional representation took on a rather different character, in some respects reminiscent of Minoan art. No longer were individual compositions so rigidly confined to a single surface, and painted decoration in particular might run continuously over more than one wall. Scenes were more often localised, with adequate background details drawn in, and besides the usual division into registers effective use was made of 'cavalier perspective', in which the ground mounts to a high horizon rather as it would appear to someone on horseback or on a hill. Time-honoured themes, especially those associated with the traditional conception of the after-life,

20  Foreign envoys

were for the most part abandoned, and even in private tombs the king and the royal family were prominently displayed, as though not only life but all eternity revolved around their persons. In palace apartments and elsewhere subjects drawn from nature were treated with great sympathy and liveliness, and intimate incidents in the domestic life of the royal household were for the first time frankly recorded (figure 9 and plates 27 and 30). Within a scene, the individual figures were often closely related through both physical and psychological contact, sometimes to an exaggerated degree (plates 27 and 30), and an overall impression of connected action successfully created. A number of new and more natural poses became common (plates 27, 30, 33 and 34) and efforts were made to express emotion and individuality, but figures were never entirely lifelike and certain conventions, such as the drawing of the eye and the variation of size according to importance, remained unchanged. There was also considerable relaxation in the greater use of sloping lines and graceful curves, and this, combined with a fondness for streamers and garlands and a sensitive appreciation of drapery (plates 27, 29, 31, 33 and 34), gave the art of Amarna a curiously feminine allure the influence of which persisted later in the New Kingdom (figure 17 and plates 35, 39, 40, 42 and 48).

The static calm of the principal figure in two-dimensional representation is closely paralleled in sculpture in the round, the two media being intimately related by reason of the sculptor's technique, based on the use of preparatory drawings. Developed during the early dynastic period, this method is essentially adapted to the carving of statues from a single block of stone, and was presumably the result of working in this material, though on the evidence at present available it might appear that the first formal figures were actually of wood.

The earliest sculptures in the round, crude manikins of clay, bone and ivory, occur in graves of predynastic date, the period immediately preceding the first dynasty being marked by a sudden advance in technique and the employment of a wider range of materials including wood, stone and faience (glazed quartz frit). It is as yet impossible to trace any broad lines of development in the work of the protodynastic period, but the small pieces that are known include a greater variety of types, and there is evidence that in wood at least larger and more advanced statues were produced. Occasional tiny statuettes of copper and amulets of gold have also survived, and an inscription records the making of a royal figure of copper, possibly on a more ambitious scale, towards the end of the second dynasty. To this same period belong the oldest extant stone statues that are unmistakably 'Egyptian' in character, the

21  Servant girl

23

elements of the dynastic style being gradually established during the third and early fourth dynasties (plates 2 and 3), when also the first sculptures of more than life-size were created. The earliest sizeable metal statue, of copper, dates from the first half of the sixth dynasty.

The initial stage in the execution of a stone statue was the drafting of sketches on at least two sides of a roughly cuboid block having as nearly as possible the dimensions and volume of the intended sculpture. As for relief and painting, preliminary guide lines and later a squared grid were generally used to ensure the correct proportioning of the body according to the canon, though the outline of the figure was not 'constructed' but drawn realistically with the side view in true profile, just as indeed stone statues were normally shown in two-dimensional representation (figure 19). The block was then systematically reduced by pounding and chipping off successive layers of stone from all sides, indispensable guide lines being drawn afresh when necessary, the technique being such that the statue possessed a certain general form throughout, though not until the final stages was it modelled in detail (figure 13). The harder stones were worked by jarring and rubbing with stone implements and by cutting with metal saws and drills used in conjunction with an abrasive, probably quartz sand, while for carving the softer stones, such as limestone, chisels and perhaps adzes with metal blades were also employed. Until the introduction of bronze in the Middle Kingdom, the sole metal available for tools was copper, and it was not until as late as the sixth century B.C. that iron came into general use for this or any other purpose.

The method practised by the Egyptian sculptor amounted in effect to the working together of the profile and frontal aspects, and as a result the finished statue retains the dense cuboid form of the parent block, remaining, as it were, imprisoned within an invisible oblong box, outside which it does not move. The median plane which divides the body lengthwise into symmetrical halves is always rigidly vertical so that as seen from the front the figure is quite straight and does not incline to either side. The line of the shoulders and hips too is rigid and almost invariably at right-angles to the vertical plane, and turning or twisting of the trunk is extremely rare, all variation of posture depending upon the treatment of the profile view, which is virtually unrestricted. But while in the case of monolithic stone statuary this characteristic stiffness is in a sense involuntary, its reiteration in sculptures of wood, metal and other materials (plates 12 and 49), where greater freedom was possible, can only be

24

due to the innate conservatism of the Egyptian craftsman or the need to fulfil some quasi-magical requirement.

Intended as a rule for the relative seclusion of a tomb or temple, Egyptian statues were designed to be seen from the front, or more rarely from the side, often against an over-powering architectural background, to which indeed their cubic mass was well adapted. The majority therefore face straight ahead, though scribes who write or read quite frequently incline towards their work and some very large sculptures glance slightly downwards with the faintest smile of gracious condescension. Less often, and always for a specific reason, the head is turned to one side, as in the case of the guardian goddesses from a shrine found in the tomb of Tutankhamūn (figure 17) and of a number of monumental lions (plate 38). With very few exceptions the standing male figure steps forward onto the left foot, while women stand with their feet together or only slightly separated (plates 6 and 7). Almost always the space between the legs of stone statues is left solid, and the legs are also united to a dorsal pillar, so that as seen from his left the striding man is apt to appear as if resting on a slope (plate 7). Seated figures of either sex in general have both legs firmly together and connected with the seat, which is often no more than a cuboid block (plates 3 and 16), and the lower limbs of squatting and kneeling individuals and those in other postures are similarly consolidated (figures 12 and 16 and plates 10, 50 and 55). The arms too are rarely separated from the body, though scribes sometimes have their elbows freed from their sides (plates 9 and 10) and there are other anomalies, notably in sculptures of the Amarna period (plates 28 and 29), and among Old Kingdom statuettes of servants, which like the minor figures in tomb scenes are on occasion quite unconventional. In the case of wooden statues and sizeable metal figures the treatment of the limbs is, on the other hand, much less restricted, largely no doubt because these were commonly made in sections and jointed together, while smaller statuettes in metal were cast from moulds formed on beeswax models. The legs are thus worked as independent units and the arms may hang free or be extended away from the body (plates 11, 12 and 49), but as in stone the basic 'frontality' is normally preserved — though some figures in Middle Kingdom tomb models and a few small pieces of New Kingdom date are naturally posed with balanced movement of the hips and shoulders. Wooden sculptures, which presented peculiar problems owing to the poor quality and difficult grain of much Egyptian timber, were carved like the softer stones with chisels and adzes, while metal statues were cast solid if small, and if large either hollow cast or hammered from sheet.

The human form is always more or less idealised in Egyptian statuary, the perfect condition implying the perpetuation of the stability and vigour of the prime of life. Men therefore preserve the virile strength and confident dignity of early middle age (plates 3, 6, 7 and 20) or, less often, are invested with the prosperous flesh of complacent seniority (plates 10 and 11) with stylised rolls of fat at the waist, while women retain the firm breasts, slim hips and graceful curves of youth (plates 6, 7, 39, 43, 44 and 49). Gross fatness, senility, disease and physical abnormality were naturally abhorrent and are not as a rule portrayed — though a very few statues of individuals with obvious congenital deformities have in fact survived (figure 15) — and children, even the youngest, tend to appear as adults on a smaller scale (figure 15). In general only the essentials are elaborated, the upper part of the body being more carefully executed than the legs and feet, which are often quite summarily treated, particularly when the figure is kneeling or squatting (plates 3 and 10), and are in other cases disproportionately large. But although the torso may be sculptured less schematically, it is never wholly naturalistic, and even in the best work its possibilities as an independent artistic unit are not realised.

The modelling of the head is usually better than that of the rest of the figure, and lifelike effects were often obtained by careful colouring and by the insertion of elaborate artificial eyes, especially during the Old Kingdom (plates 3, 9, 10, 11, 26 and 32). Frequently too there seems to have been a real attempt to reproduce the actual features of the person represented, but facial expression is generally absent, and most statues gaze blankly into eternity with, at best, a vague smile of benign vacuity. Occasionally, however, as in some royal portraits of the Middle Kingdom (figure 14 and plates 17 and 18), the face has an air of individuality, and the sculptor seems even to have achieved a measure of success in the difficult task of delineating character. But the quality of the portrait was always in a sense irrelevant, for the identity of any statue was ultimately assured by the inscription of the person's name (plates 3, 7 and 20), and the erasure or alteration of that name was adequate to destroy or change the identity of a figure without any further attempt to modify the features (plates 19 and 37). The portrait head or bust as such had, moreover, no place in Egyptian sculpture, for, being incomplete, it could not properly fulfil the magical function of an entire statue. The only known example, of fourth dynasty date, was perhaps incorporated in the decoration of a tomb chapel, while of the many realistic heads and masks of the Amarna period none is in fact a finished product. Some, like the quartzite heads of Nefertiti and the princesses (figure 10), were elements of composite statues, designed to be fitted into bodies of different materials, while others, including the well-known polychrome head of the queen (plate 32), were studio portraits intended merely to be used as models for future sculptures (figure 11).

The tendency of the Egyptian sculptor to concentrate on essentials may be seen as the first step towards a conscious simplification of form, and the gradual movement in this direction was inevitably accelerated during the Middle Kingdom, when statues were for the first time virtually mass produced for a less exclusive and discriminating patronage. Of the private sculptures of this period, standing, seated and squatting alike, many were conceived as enveloped in a long mantle from which only the head, hands and feet protrude (plate 16) — a convention recalling that of the earliest royal representations — while a new and very formalised type, the so-called block statue, was introduced. This latter, in which the figure, squatting on its haunches, is reduced to little more than a shaped block with the flat surface of the shins providing an ideal ground for inscription (figure 16), became increasingly common during the New Kingdom, together with another type of similar compactness — that of the kneeling votary supporting a shrine, offering table or stela (figure 12). Colossal statuary too was often simplified in harmony with its architectural setting, and naturalism was also sacrificed in the treatment of monumental lions and other animal sculptures (plates 19, 38 and 51). Sometimes, however, and to an ever greater extent in the work of the Saite period (twenty-sixth dynasty) and later, the subordination of the subject is quite independent of any such considerations, and seems to stem from a genuine appreciation of the possibilities of purely formal composition and a simple desire to create an aesthetically pleasing shape (plates 52 and 54).

One of the outstanding characteristics of Egyptian sculpture is the sureness with which even the most refractory materials have been mastered, a sureness already demonstrated in the manufacture of hard stone vases in the predynastic and proto-dynastic periods. Though many were originally destined to be daubed in bold and uncompromising colours, and so to have their finer detail as well as the qualities of the stone obliterated, the best examples of Egyptian statuary bear testimony to the sculptor's instinctive feeling for the natural beauty and decorative possibilities of his material. Even during the Old Kingdom, when sculpture seems always to have been painted either wholly or in part, ornamental stones, brought from the remotest quarries, were laboriously worked and finished, despite the fact that surface niceties would disappear beneath the pigment. From the Middle Kingdom onwards, however, and increasingly in the New Kingdom and later, though alabaster, limestone and sandstone were still as a rule painted, sculptures in the harder rocks such as basalt, diorite, granite, quartzite and 'schist' (greywacke) were frequently left untouched or only partially coloured (plates 37 and 47), so that the full potentialities of the different stones could be explored (plates 18, 51, 53, 54 and 55). Subtle variation was realised in the treatment of surface texture, smoothness and high polish being contrasted with decorative patterning and delicacy of detail in the modelling of individual features (plates 20, 44, 51, 52 and 54), while deliberate use was, on occasion, made of the natural veining of the stone. An inscription of Ramses II boasts indeed that statues of black granite with crowns of quartzite were extracted from a quarry near Aswan, and though as yet no actual example has been discovered there are in fact at least three sculptures of this same pharaoh in which the natural faulting of black and red granite has been turned to advantage (plate 47). In the Amarna period the decorative use of coloured stones — of varying shades of quartzite for example — was often exaggerated, and statues were sometimes composed of separate elements worked in stones of the appropriate colour or even in faience and glass (figure 10 and plate 26), though such pieces were a novelty, and opposed to the normal Egyptian practice of carving statues from a single block.

The Egyptian craftsman's feeling for the materials with which he worked and his appreciation of form and beauty are nowhere more clearly revealed than in the field of applied art, since the making of objects which had in the main no re-creative purpose was not inhibited by the same beliefs which conditioned the approach to statuary and two-dimensional representation. That anything made should serve a practical end, either in this life or the next, was taken for granted, the production of a few *objets d'art* without apparent function for the affluent society of the late eighteenth dynasty being exceptional, but beyond this the artisan was influenced only by tradition, with frequent opportunities for the exercise of personal ingenuity.

In a country rich in gold, electrum and semi-precious stones the art of the jeweller flourished from an early date, and several notable examples of gold work have survived from the protodynastic period and from the Old Kingdom. It was, however, during the twelfth dynasty that the most tasteful jewellery was created, the inlaid diadems, pendants, bracelets and other pieces from a few rich burials of this time being quite unsurpassed by later work in quality of design, though not perhaps in execution. From a purely technical standpoint indeed the best work of the New Kingdom is possibly more accomplished, and in some instances of unparalleled splendour (plate 36), but the aesthetic effect is often impaired by a certain lack of restraint, and many of the ornaments of the late eighteenth and nineteenth dynasties are in fact somewhat

28

vulgar. Until about the beginning of the eighteenth dynasty the use of silver was comparatively rare, and its value greater than that of gold, while lapis lazuli, the most prized of all the semi-precious stones, had always to be imported. Jewellery apart, the level of metalworking was generally high, especially during the New Kingdom and later, and not only finely detailed figures (plate 49) but graceful vessels and a variety of other objects were made in precious and base metals. The extensive use of metal (usually gold) foil and leaf for overlaying furniture (plate 34), coffins and even architectural features may also be noted, some very refined work being carried out on a base of modelled plaster.

The material known as Egyptian faience — which is not true faience but an alkaline glazed quartz frit — was introduced during the predynastic period, and in dynastic times was widely employed not only as a substitute for semi-precious stones in making beads, amulets, scarabs and inlay (plate 34), but also for larger things such as bowls, chalices and other vessels, statuettes, including funerary figurines (shawabtis) and tiles and similarly sizeable elements of architectural decoration. Unglazed blue frit, too, was used for beads and small objects from as early as the fourth dynasty, and to a somewhat greater extent, and on a larger scale, from the eighteenth dynasty onwards. Glass on the other hand, though occurring sporadically in earlier periods, does not appear to have been made intentionally until the New Kingdom, when it enjoyed a certain vogue, being chiefly employed, like faience, for beads and inlay (plates 34 and 36), and also for vases, as well as, more rarely, for bowls, statuettes and other purposes. From the end of the twentieth dynasty, however, the popularity of glass declined, its disuse to some extent coinciding with the development of a new material, 'glassy faience', the composition of which was somewhere between that of faience and glass.

The carpenter's craft, though always rather hampered by the scarcity of good timber, was already advanced in the protodynastic period, as is shown by the extant fragments of statuary and furniture, and was in many respects fully developed by the middle of the Old Kingdom. In the Middle Kingdom, however, and again during the eighteenth and nineteenth dynasties, cabinet-making attained new levels of excellence, and boxes, chairs, beds and other articles of furniture were often elaborately decorated with veneer, inlay and marquetry (plates 34 and 35). On a smaller scale, elegant trinket caskets, cosmetic spoons and similar toilet accessories, as well as gaming pieces and the handles of sticks and whips, were expertly carved in both wood and ivory and minutely painted and inlaid.

The technique of stone vase manufacture was sophisticated as early as the pre-

22  Acrobatic dancing girl

23 Girl musician

24 Girl painting her lips

dynastic period, when sculpture in stone or any other material was still in its infancy, and the industry indeed reached its peak during the first three dynasties, when vessels of graceful form were painstakingly worked in the hardest rocks. Less difficult materials such as alabaster and serpentine were increasingly preferred from the fourth dynasty onwards, and while shapes became more complicated the quality of finish of the earlier work was hardly equalled, except perhaps by some cosmetic jars of the Middle Kingdom. A like decline may also be remarked in the case of Egyptian pottery, the most pleasing pieces belonging to the Badarian and predynastic periods, whereas dynastic pottery, even when painted as sometimes in the New Kingdom, is generally less effective.

Of the remaining crafts none can properly be included under the heading of applied art, though decorative leatherwork with embossed, punched and appliqué designs was not uncommon during the New Kingdom. Occasional examples of tapestry and warp woven textiles and of embroidered fabrics are also known from the same period, and baskets of this date were often ornamented with patterns worked out in stitching or coloured fibres.

Passing reference has already been made to the purely decorative use of painting, notably in the patterning of ceilings where striking motifs of rich design and colour are often to be found, this aspect of the draughtsman's craft being of course quite unaffected by the requirements of re-creative representation. Similarly untrammelled are the sketches made on flakes of limestone (ostraca), the majority dating from the New Kingdom, which seem in many cases to have been mere 'doodles' done for pleasure (figures 22 and 23). The subjects, drawn freehand, often quite delicately, and sometimes painted (figure 22), are very varied, certain favourite themes, however, recurring with some frequency, and details occasionally being copied from tomb and temple scenes (figure 5). Unconventional drawings of this kind were also executed on papyrus, though comparatively few fragments have in fact survived, the most complete example including sketches of animals and an erotic sequence (figure 24).

# NOTES ON THE ILLUSTRATIONS

In the following descriptions measurements are given to the nearest quarter of an inch or half centimetre. The term 'statuette' is applied to figures of less than one-third life-size (2 ft or 60 cm. for a standing figure), and 'colossus' to those over one and one-third times life-size (8 ft or 2 m. 40 cm. for a standing figure).

## BLACK AND WHITE ILLUSTRATIONS

**Figure 1** (Frontispiece) *Naos-stela of the sculptor Bak*. Quartzite. Height 2 ft 1 in. (63.5 cm.). Amarna period. Staatliche Museen, Berlin-Dahlem.
The chief sculptor (*seankh*), 'the assistant of his majesty', Bak and his wife Tahere are portrayed in the manner of the early years of the Amarna period, the man's exaggerated paunch (see figure 18) protruding even beyond the front of the niche. Like his father Men, who perhaps created the famous 'Memnon' colossi, Bak was overseer of works in the quartzite quarries, and may have been partly responsible for the frequent use of this material at Amarna. The stela, in the same stone, will surely have been made under his personal supervision, if not by his own hand, and the figure of the sculptor may thus be regarded as a self-portrait.

**Figure 2** *The sculptor Iuti at work*. Limestone carved in sunk relief. Height of figure 4½ in. (11.5 cm.). Amarna period. In the tomb of Huya at Amarna.
The overseer of sculptors to queen Tiy is seen putting the finishing touches to a statue of the princess Baketaten, while other 'sculptors' (*seankh*) work on a head, presumably for a composite statue, and the leg of a chair or bed. The figures are represented in true profile, but in the Amarna style (see plate 27), the disproportionately large head given to Iuti, and the fact that his name is written twice, perhaps suggesting that this is a self-portrait.

**Figure 3** *Tutankhamūn victorious over the Nubians*. Painting on gesso plaster over wood. Length of scene about 1 ft 8 in. (50 cm.). Late eighteenth dynasty. From the tomb of Tutankhamūn at Thebes. Egyptian Museum, Cairo.
Though on so small a scale, this scene from the side of a box, framed by a decorative border, exhibits many of the features typical of an Egyptian battle scene, the action being concentrated in an enlarged hieroglyph of victory — in this case wishful, since Tutankhamūn conducted no such campaign. The boy king, drawn on a larger scale and in a calm, heroic pose, triumphs over the enemy horde almost single-handed, the supporting chariotry taking no part in the fight, while the foot-soldiers merely administer the *coup de grâce*. The contrast between order and chaos is accentuated by the use of registers to separate the attendant Egyptian chariots, whereas the mass of the slain mounts to a high horizon, with the bodies twisted at all angles and several shown full-face. Two vultures symbolically protect the king, with between them the sun disk flanked by cobras from which depend the sign of life, and above them the heaven, represented hieroglyphically. The king's name and a brief 'caption' fill the remaining space. The painting is varnished, and there appears to be shading on the king's horses, which rear across the centre of the composition creating a diagonal division.

**Figure 4** *Ramses III hunting wild cattle*. Sandstone, carved in sunk relief, with traces of painting over plaster. Figure of king about life-size. Twentieth dynasty. In the temple of Medinet Habu at Thebes.
Representative of the sunk relief decoration of Ramessid temples, this detail from a hunting scene depicts the pursuit of wild cattle in the reeds bordering a stretch of water, the setting being an integral part of the representation. The king, attended only by a troop of soldiers shown below on a smaller scale, is calm and poised, while the bulls, naturalistically portrayed with even the horns of two correctly drawn, fall contorted before him. The line of the bank and the patch of reeds, more or less conventionally drawn, rise to a high horizon, and fish and birds, represented almost as hieroglyphs, are

crowded on the water. Purely symbolic is the falcon placed protectively above the king (see figure 3), before which the substance of the action is related in columns of text.

**Figure 5** *The chief of Pwenet and his consort.* Limestone, carved in low relief and painted. Height of queen 1 ft 1 in. (33 cm.). Early eighteenth dynasty. From the temple of Deir el Bahari at Thebes. Egyptian Museum, Cairo.
Though the figures are conventionally constructed — with, however, the hands correctly paired — the enormous pathological fatness of the chieftain's wife and her obviously un-Egyptian features have been successfully captured (see figure 20). The block belongs to the record of queen Hatshepsut's expedition to Pwenet (? on the Somali coast), from which the detail of the grotesque woman was sketched on a flake of limestone, some three centuries later.

**Figure 6** *Drawing board with canonical master-drawing.* Drawing on gesso over wood. Length 1 ft 9 in. (53.5 cm.). Mid eighteenth dynasty. From an unknown tomb at Thebes. British Museum, London.
The chief interest of the drawing board lies in the representation of a seated king, Thutmose III (see plate 20), outlined in black over a preliminary sketch in red, and inscribed within a squared grid — an explicit example of a figure constructed in accordance with the first canon of proportion. Originally the grid covered the whole board and contained a second seated figure to the right, but this was erased in antiquity and replaced by a drawing of a quail chick and a series of sketches illustrating basic units of linear measurement. The canon to which the figure conforms is that which prevailed from early dynastic times until the Saite period (twenty-sixth dynasty), when, as a consequence of metrological reforms, the system was altered in such a way that the constructed proportions of the body no longer corresponded to those of nature.

**Figure 7** *Sculptor's trial piece.* Sketch on limestone, partly carved in sunk relief. Height 9 in. (23 cm.). Amarna period. From Amarna. Egyptian Museum, Cairo.
An easy freehand sketch, emended in places, has been only partially carved in sunk relief, the torso remaining roughly modelled, while the legs and feet — which, like the hands, are correctly represented (see plates 27 and 30) — appear to be virtually finished. The piece is probably a sculptor's trial study, though like others it may have been designed as a decorative plaque (see plate 33).

**Figure 8** *Unfinished decoration in a tomb.* Outline drawing on limestone, partly carved in low relief. Figures about one-quarter life-size. Late eighteenth dynasty. In the tomb of Horemheb at Thebes.
A sudden cessation of work has here preserved a number of different stages in the execution of relief. Both preliminary and corrected drawings, largely freehand, are clearly visible — the figure in the stern of the barque has been sketched three times — and the carving of different elements is variously advanced. Figures at the base of the scene are completed, individual hieroglyphs are carved in detail, cut out as flat shapes, or not even begun, and the god in the shrine is almost finished about the face yet largely untouched below (see figure 7).

**Figure 9** *Unfinished relief.* Limestone, carved in low relief. Height 6¾ in. (17 cm.). Amarna period. From Amarna. Staatliche Museen zu Berlin.
This small plaque, perhaps intended as a piece of architectural inlay (see plate 33), dates from the closing years of the Amarna period, and represents Akhenaten (seated) with his co-regent Smenkhkarē. The sculptor has almost finished cutting round the outline drawing and reducing the background, so that the figures stand out sharply in flat relief, but as yet without any surface modelling.

**Figure 10** *Unfinished head.* Quartzite. Height 1 ft 1 in. (33 cm.). Amarna period. From Amarna. Egyptian Museum, Cairo.
The tang projecting at the base of the neck, the absence of ears and the rough surface left to receive a wig of another material show that the head (? of queen Nefertiti) was intended for a composite statue. The work is near to completion — the lips have already been painted, presumably to judge the effect — but even at this stage there are guide lines indicating the median plane of the face and the line of the hair. The eyes and eyebrows are also rather coarsely marked, and were evidently destined to be cut out and inlaid.

**Figure 11** *Sculptor's trial study of a head.* Limestone. Height 11½ in. (29 cm.). Amarna period. From Amarna. Staatliche Museen zu Berlin.
Rough corrections, most clearly visible on the left side of the face and neck, suggest that this was a trial study by an apprentice working under the supervision of a master sculptor. The piece was found in the same workshop as the famous polychrome head of Nefertiti (see plate 32) and was in all probability copied from it.

**Figure 12** *Unfinished statue.* Limestone. Height 1 ft 5 in. (43 cm.). Ptolemaic period. From Tanis. Egyptian Museum, Cairo.

The obviously carved surface of this sculpture, which dates from a period when iron chisels were in common use, is in marked contrast to the appearance of most unfinished statues of earlier date (see figure 13). The work is also irregular, the right side of the figure being much further advanced than the left side, which is merely roughed out.

**Figure 13** *Unfinished statue*. Limestone. Height 1 ft 4½ in. (42 cm.). Amarna Period. From Amarna. Egyptian Museum, Cairo.
The uniform advancement of the whole sculpture and the 'pitted' appearance of the surface, with guide lines still in evidence, are characteristic of most unfinished statuary. The pose of the group, though not entirely without parallel, is unusual in its coherence, the head of the smaller figure being turned naturally to face the other (see figure 17). The piece is generally taken to represent Akhenaten dandling one of his daughters, but the suggestion that it may portray the acceptance of Smenkhkarē as co-regent is worth noting.

**Figure 14** *Head of a statue of Senwosret III*. Obsidian. Height 5 in. (13 cm.). Twelfth dynasty. Gulbenkian Foundation, Lisbon.
Perhaps the most expressive of all Middle Kingdom royal portraits, this fragment, expertly carved in obsidian, is the more remarkable for the sculptor's controlled mastery of a refractory material. The head was formerly thought to represent Amenemhet III (see plates 18 and 19), but the brooding features are now recognised as those of his father and predecessor Senwosret III (see plate 17).

**Figure 15** *Statuette of the dwarf Seneb and his family*. Limestone, painted. Height 1 ft 1 in. (33 cm.). Late fifth — sixth dynasty. From Giza. Egyptian Museum, Cairo.
The group of the dwarf Seneb and his family, one of the few sculptures of a deformed person, is of particular interest for the way in which the equilibrium of an ordinary dyad (a statue of two persons) has been maintained. The little man, realistically portrayed, perches cross-legged on the bench beside his quite normal wife who supports him with a conventional embrace (see plate 6), while the two children occupy the space which the dwarfed lower limbs could not be made to fill. The rounded child figures, though somewhat stylised, are less like those of miniature adults than is usual, and the pose of the woman is made less rigid by a slight torsion of the upper part of the body.

**Figure 16** *Block statue of Sennefer*. Granite. Height 2 ft 10 in. (86 cm.). Mid eighteenth dynasty. From Thebes. British Museum, London.

The basic form of the block statue, with the body reduced to a smooth contoured mass and the surface of the shins adapted as a ground for inscriptions, is here fairly typified — though the degree of attention given to the feet and hands will often vary. In this case the head is quite stylised, but in other examples the detail of the face and wig is very different from the summary treatment of the body, suggesting perhaps that figures were sometimes ready-made, with only the head to be completed for the patron.

**Figure 17** *Statue of the goddess Selket*. Wood, gilded. Height 2 ft 11¾ in. (91 cm.). Late eighteenth dynasty. From the tomb of Tutankhamūn at Thebes. Egyptian Museum, Cairo.
This charming goddess, identified by the hieroglyph which crowns her head (see plate 7), is one of four which flanked a shrine. The delicately draped figure, with its curious Amarna allure (see plates 29 and 39), is treated with considerable freedom, the arms gracefully extended in a gesture of protection and the head turned to one side so as not to face directly into the wall of the shrine.

**Figure 18** *Colossal statue of Akhenaten*. Sandstone, with traces of painting. Rather more than twice life-size. Amarna period. From the temple area of Karnak at Thebes. Egyptian Museum, Cairo.
This broken colossus, its legs missing below the knees, is the best preserved of several recovered from the ruins of a temple of the Aten at Karnak. The grotesque exaggeration of the figure — almost a caricature, with its gaunt features, full hips and protruding paunch — is typical of the earlier phase of the Amarna 'revolution', and, while it may possibly reflect actual physical abnormality in the king, it seems more likely to be symbolic of his identification with the fecund, life-giving Aten. The sculpture is in sandstone, a material not much used for statuary unless on a large scale.

**Figure 19** *Stonemasons at work*. Painting on limestone. Height of seated statue about 1 ft 8 in. (50 cm.). Mid eighteenth dynasty. In the tomb of Rekhmirē at Thebes.
In this detail, sculptors are shown engaged on two colossal scaffolded statues of granite (painted in imitation) and a sphinx and offering table of limestone, the tools used being evidently of stone. Successive stages of the work are seen taking place simultaneously, but the statues, drawn in true profile, are represented as already finished — a convention strikingly paralleled in a well-known scene of the transport of a colossus, where the statue is shown complete although in the accompanying text it is described as 'a squared block as it came from the rock face'. The attempt to depict the workmen in natural poses has been variously successful, with rather

inept drafting of the shoulders in most cases, and the back view of the head and torso of the bending figure is quite unusual.

**Figure 20** *Foreign envoys*. Outline drawing on limestone. About two-thirds life-size. Amarna period. In the tomb of Ramose at Thebes.
The group is part of a scene in which the vizier is shown receiving courtiers and foreign emissaries, and is remarkable for the skilful characterisation of the different racial types. The decoration of this part of the wall was carried out during the Amarna period (when true profile was comparatively common) and was never completed; the outline drawing which survives having been intended as the first sketch for a relief (see plate 25).

**Figure 21** *Servant girl*. Painting on limestone. Height of figure 1 ft 5½ in. (44.5 cm.). Mid eighteenth dynasty. In the tomb of Rekhmirē at Thebes.
The scene from which this figure is taken, though unusually sober in colouring, is dextrously drawn, with many of the servant girls depicted in true profile. The extraordinary three-quarter back view here attempted is quite convincingly handled, save for the impossible placing of the feet, shown as though the figure were normally posed — an error unconsciously rectified in several early hand reproductions of this detail.

**Figure 22** *Acrobatic dancing girl*. Painted sketch on limestone. Height of figure 3 in. (7.5 cm.). Late eighteenth dynasty. From Thebes. Museo Egizio, Turin.
The attempt to sketch a lively and unusual pose has resulted in an unnatural elongation of the body, and notably of the arms. The hands and feet are accurately drawn and the fall of the hair is realistic, but the line of the throat does not coincide with that of the breast, and — a small detail — the earring is drawn in place despite the position of the head. Though the majority of painted ostraca belong to the nineteenth and twentieth dynasties, the style of this drawing and its fineness, as well as the type of 'loincloth' of slit leather worn by the dancer (see figure 3), suggest that it is to be dated to the latter part of the eighteenth.

**Figure 23** *Girl musician*. Sketch on limestone. Height of figure 4 in. (10 cm.). Nineteenth dynasty. From Deir el Medina, Thebes. Staatliche Museen zu Berlin.
The free and unconventional drawing of the figure, with the body full-face and the head, turned away, in profile, is common to several similar sketches of girl musicians and dancers and may also be paralleled in more formal representations (see plates 21 and 24). The sure outlines follow a preliminary sketch in red, the style

of the work, as well as the choice of subject, indicating that the piece belongs to the early nineteenth dynasty.

**Figure 24** *Girl painting her lips*. Sketch on papyrus. Height of figure 3¼ in. (8.5 cm.). Twentieth dynasty. From Thebes. Museo Egizio, Turin.
Remarkable as one of the very few Egyptian representations of a person actually looking into a mirror, this detail is taken from one of an interesting series of erotic sketches. The figure, half squatting with the knees raised, is drawn, as in another of the scenes, with the whole of the body viewed from the front and only the head seen in profile. The mirror is held up in front of the face, but so as to be recognisable is turned flat — so that, in effect, the girl is looking into its edge.

# COLOUR PLATES

**Plate 1** *Panel of Hesirē*. Wood, carved in low relief. Height 3 ft 9¼ in. (1 m. 15 cm.). Third dynasty. From the tomb of Hesirē at Sakkara. Egyptian Museum, Cairo.
The figure on this sculptured panel, one of eleven found in the tomb, exemplifies the conventional form of the standing male 'constructed' according to the canon. The relief, although in wood, is finely executed, with the musculature of the body well modelled, the hands correctly represented, and the detail of the wig and pleated kilt, as well as the accompanying hieroglyphs minutely carved. The nobleman carries the staff and sceptre indicative of his rank, together with a palette and pen case to symbolise his position of royal scribe (see plates 9 and 10). Though the face, with its strong nose and small moustache (see plate 3), may be a portrait, the identity is effectively established by the addition of the name and titles above.

**Plate 2** *Statue of the princess Redidjet*. Diorite. Height 2 ft 8¾ in. (83 cm.). Third dynasty. Possibly from Sakkara. Museo Egizio, Turin.
The statue is one of a small number of sculptures, similar in style, which belong to the period of the late second and early third dynasties. The full wig, the simple dress with deeply cleft neckline, and the position of the left hand are common to all the female figures of the group, while the form of the seat, reproducing a simple wooden stool — in this case with a low back rest — is also characteristic. The handling of the stone, though perhaps lacking finesse, is quite assured, both in the overall modelling of the piece and in the more careful carving of the wig and face.

**Plate 3** *Statues of the prince Rahotpe and his wife Nofret.* Limestone, painted. Height 3 ft 11¼ in. (1 m. 20 cm.) and 3 ft 10½ in. (1 m. 18 cm.). Fourth dynasty. From Medum. Egyptian Museum, Cairo.

The finished appearance of a properly painted and inscribed limestone sculpture is remarkably preserved in these two seated statues so closely related as almost to constitute a dyad (see plate 6). The flesh of the man is coloured brown, less reddish than is often the case, and that of the woman a creamy yellow, with the hair of both and the latter's artificial wig black, and other details in appropriate tints. The inlaid eyes are of the most elaborate type (see plates 9 and 11), the eyelids being of copper, the white of quartz, the cornea of rock crystal, the iris of a brownish material, probably resin, with a darker pupil, and the caruncles painted. The heads are evidently idealised portraits, the prince, with his cropped hair and short moustache — perhaps a sign of nobility (see plate 1) — appearing the more lifelike. The treatment of the bodies is also quite successful, the prince's heavy shoulders possibly reproducing a characteristic of the royal house to which he belonged (see plates 6 and 7), but the lower limbs of both, and particularly the lady's ankles, are less carefully handled.

**Plate 4** *Geese in a marsh.* Painting on plaster. Height of geese about 8 in. (20 cm.). Fourth dynasty. From the tomb of Itet at Medum. Egyptian Museum, Cairo.

The line of geese from which these details are taken was originally part of a rural scene including the trapping of birds in a marsh (see plate 15, here conventionally indicated by tufts of rush. Though stiffly posed, the geese, of three different species, are carefully detailed, and their colouring is more subtle and closer to nature than in most later work. It was in this same tomb that experiment was made with the curious technique of 'painting' by filling carved outlines with solid masses of pigment.

**Plate 5** *Slab-stela of the princess Nofretiabet.* Limestone, carved in low relief and painted. Height 1 ft 2¾ in. (37.5 cm.). Fourth dynasty. From Giza. Musée du Louvre, Paris.

Though not perhaps one of the most accomplished examples of Old Kingdom relief sculpture, the stela is notable for the excellent preservation of the original painting with its finely drawn detail. The princess, clad in a dress imitating leopard skin, her name written above her head, is seated before an offering table which is little more than an enlarged hieroglyph. Above and beside are listed various items of food and drink, cosmetics and linen cloth, the hieroglyphs, in typically neat groupings, being faithfully coloured and deftly outlined.

**Plates 6 and 7** *Statue of Menkaurē and queen Khamerernebty.* Schist, with traces of painting. Height 4 ft 7 in. (1 m. 39.5 cm.). Fourth dynasty. From Giza. Museum of Fine Arts, Boston. *Statue of Menkaurē between two goddesses.* Schist, with traces of painting. Height 3 ft 1 in. (94 cm.). Fourth dynasty. From Giza. Egyptian Museum, Cairo.

The stance of the king in the Boston dyad, one of the earliest known, is typical of the standing male statue, the long stride contrasting with the short step of the queen, who supports her husband with a gesture which later becomes common (see figure 15). The figures are idealised, though the king's massive shoulders may be characteristic (see plate 3) and his facial features evidently approximate to a portrait. The sculpture was never completed, the lower limbs remaining unpolished and the base and dorsal slab being quite rough and without inscription, but traces of pigment indicate that the group was coloured.

In the triad, one of four similar groups preserved intact, the king is supported by the goddess Hathor, on his right, and a goddess representing the district of Cynopolis. The stance and treatment of the figures is similar, but the work is finished, with considerable traces of the final painting preserved. Inscriptions on the base serve to identify the trio, and the goddesses are further distinguished by the symbols on their heads (see figure 17), Hathor having sun disk and horns (see plate 42) and her companion the standard of the region she personifies.

**Plate 8** *Herdsmen with cattle.* Limestone, carved in low relief and painted. Height of the rear man about 1 ft (30 cm.). Fifth dynasty. In the tomb of Thy at Sakkara.

While not as polished as the best work of the fourth dynasty, the relief decoration of the tomb of Thy is distinguished for the liveliness of its compositions, well illustrated by this detail from an agricultural scene. If the drafting of the youths is not wholly successful, the cattle, viewed in profile save for their horns, are naturalistically modelled, the varied attitudes of the leading group and the backward glance of the calf creating interest and a certain unity. The representation of the water, through which the legs are visible, is an ingenious compromise, showing in fact the surface, with stylised ripples, yet at the same time indicating depth (see plates 22 and 23). The hieroglyphs, supplying the words of the herdsmen, are an integral part of the scene.

**Plates 9 and 10** *Statue of an official in the rôle of scribe.* Limestone, painted. Height 1 ft 8 in. (51 cm.), Fifth dynasty. From Sakkara. Egyptian Museum, Cairo. *Statue of an official in the rôle of scribe.* Limestone painted. Height 1 ft 8¾ in. (53 cm.). Fifth dynasty. From Sakkara. Musée du Louvre, Paris.

The symbolic representation of court officials in the guise of scribes was common during the Old Kingdom, and may perhaps indicate the holding of some nominal position (see plates 1 and 46). The subject of the well-known Louvre sculpture, which retains much of its original colouring, is portrayed as prosperously corpulent, with the folds of the fleshy body and the sharp line of the collar-bone realistically modelled. The legs and feet are less well executed, but the treatment of the hands is remarkably natural, and the head, with its close-cropped hair, strong bony features and inlaid eyes, is almost alive.

The statue from which the detail is taken is that of a less portly, and perhaps younger man, also posed as a scribe but with poorly sculptured legs and feet. The face, framed by a full wig, lacks the alertness of the other, but the expression is more subtle and the total effect no less convincing. The inlaid eyes (and probably also those of the Louvre sculpture) are similar to those of Rahotpe and Nofret (see plate 3).

**Plates 11 and 12** *Statue of an official.* Wood, originally painted over plaster. Height 3ft 7¼ in. (1 m. 10 cm.). Fifth dynasty. From Sakkara. Egyptian Museum, Cairo. *Statue of Methethy.* Wood, painted over plaster. Height 2 ft 11 in. (89 cm.). Late fifth — sixth dynasty. From Sakkara. Brooklyn Museum, New York.

During the Old Kingdom it was not unusual for individuals to be represented by pairs of statues, one having a short kilt and wig, the other a longer garment and close-cropped hair. The Cairo figure, ascribed to Kaaperu, is of the latter type, portraying realistically a man no longer young, with fleshy face and neck and rotund body — the legs and feet and the staff are restored. The disappearance of the coating of plaster and paint reveals the method of jointing the arms and also the skilled modelling of the head, enlivened with elaborate inlaid eyes (see plate 3).

The statue of Methethy, one of five that are known, is of the type with kilt and wig and is excellently preserved, illustrating well the original appearance of a painted wooden sculpture. The figure is, however, idealised and technically inferior to the other, the roughly finished wood being covered with three layers of plaster of different qualities, in which the finer details of the body and the curls of the wig are modelled. The use of wood for statuary was to some extent a substitution, since it had not the permanence of stone, though for the sculptor it was often no less difficult to work.

**Plates 13 and 14** *Senwosret I and the god Min.* Limestone, carved in sunk relief. Height 4 ft 7 in. (1 m. 40 cm.). Twelfth dynasty. From Coptos. University College, London. *Senwosret I and the god Ptah.* Limestone, carved in low relief. Height 11 ft (3 m. 35 cm.). Twelfth dynasty. From the temple of Karnak at Thebes. Egyptian Museum, Cairo.

The close relationship between representation and inscription is clearly apparent in the drafting of these two ritual scenes, of which the hieroglyphs form an essential part. Plate 13, a fine example of sunk relief, depicts Senwosret running before Min, the well modelled musculature of the striding king and his vigorous, though stylised, action being in marked contrast to the stiff attitude of the god.

The scene on plate 14, from a pillar, is in comparatively bold low relief, the cutting clear and precise, and shows the god Ptah within his shrine embracing the king (see plate 42), whose pose is static and conventional. In neither case have more than slight traces of the original painting survived.

**Plate 15** *Birds in an acacia tree.* Painting on limestone. Height 1 ft 10 in. (56 cm.). Twelfth dynasty. In the tomb of Khnemhotpe at Beni Hasan.

The subject is part of a scene in which the owner of the tomb is shown netting ducks in the marshes, the edge of the water appearing schematically on the right (see plates 22 and 23), with the heads of several ducks and the border of the net above. The acacia tree in flower — balanced by another beyond the marsh — is quite faithfully represented, and the birds which perch in it are readily identified as a hoopoe, three shrikes and a redstart.

**Plate 16** *Statue of Khertyhotpe.* Quartzite. Height 2 ft 5½ in. (75 cm.). Twelfth dynasty. From Asyut. Staatliche Museen zu Berlin.

Crisply executed in the hardest stone worked by the Egyptians, this statue is one of the most accomplished private sculptures of the Middle Kingdom. The combination of a simplified body with a carefully detailed head is typical of many works of this period, the more or less idealised portrait being frequently influenced, as here, by the contemporary royal type (see plates 17, 18 and 19).

**Plates 17 and 18** *Head of a statue of Senwosret III.* Granite. Height 1 ft 1¼ in. (33.5 cm.). Twelfth dynasty. Fitzwilliam Museum, Cambridge. *Head of a statue of Amenemhet III.* Serpentine. Height 5 in. (12.5 cm.). Twelfth dynasty. Fitzwilliam Museum, Cambridge.

The Egyptian sculptor's skill in handling different materials and his ability to achieve a convincing portrait regardless of size are well illustrated by these two royal heads of the later Middle Kingdom. The dour, rather melancholy traits of the sadly battered granite statue, of more than life-size, are clearly recognisable as those of Senwosret III (see figure 14), while the highly polished serpentine fragment, from a much smaller sculpture, has the slightly idealised features and reflective expression of his son and successor, Amenemhet III, as a young man.

**Plate 19** *Sphinx of Amenemhet III.* Granite. Length 7 ft 4½ in. (2 m. 25 cm.). Twelfth dynasty. From Tanis. Egyptian Museum, Cairo.

Although the original inscription has been erased and the piece three times usurped, the king here represented as a sphinx is almost certainly to be identified as Amenemhet III (see plate 18). The form of the sphinx is unusual in that only the face is human, the customary *nemes* headdress (see plates 18 and 20) being replaced by an elaborately stylised lion's mane and ears — the latter restored (see plate 38).

**Plate 20** *Statue of Thutmose III.* Schist. Height 2 ft 11½ in. (90 cm.). Mid eighteenth dynasty. From the temple of Karnak at Thebes. Egyptian Museum, Cairo.

The Egyptian ideal of manhood and kingship is typified in this small statue of the energetic warrior Thutmose III, formally posed and wearing the *nemes* headdress and pleated kilt of royalty (see plates 6 and 14). The execution of the piece is very refined, both in the smooth sculpturing of the body surface and the crisp carving of the false beard, headdress and linen garment. The figure is identified by the name on the waistband, and the features, though somewhat idealised, are characteristic, a certain softness in the benign smile being perhaps a legacy from the reign of Thutmose's predecessor, queen Hatshepsut.

**Plate 21** *Guests and musicians at a banquet.* Painting on plaster. Height of harpist about 1 ft 4 in. (40 cm.). Mid eighteenth dynasty. In the tomb of Nakht at Thebes.

In the banqueting scene from which these details are taken, the female entertainers occupy the lowest register, i.e. the foreground, while the guests, seated in rows behind, are shown above (see plate 24). The latter are conventionally drawn, but the maid who serves them is in profile, while the girl with the lute below is posed in a manner common to other figures of this type (see figure 23 and plate 24), her turned head uniting the trio of musicians as that of the second lady links the group above (see plate 24). The drawing of the hands of the harpist and of the girl with the pipes is unusually realistic, and transparency seems to be suggested in the colouring of their bodies beneath their dresses. A particularly interesting feature of the painting is the use of varnish on the figures of the entertainers.

**Plates 22 and 23** *Fishing and fowling in the marshes.* Painting on plaster. Height of left figure about 2 ft 2 in. (66 cm.). Mid eighteenth dynasty. In the tomb of Menna at Thebes. *Fowling in the marshes.* Painting on plaster. Height of figure 1 ft 9½ in. (55 cm.). Mid eighteenth dynasty. From the tomb of Nebamūn at Thebes. British Museum, London.

The scene of the owner fishing and fowling in the marshes, found in a number of tombs, is suitably illustrated from that of Menna. Save for the little girl plucking a lotus, who is shown in profile, the figures are represented in the usual manner, graded in size according to their importance, with the principals duplicated on either side of the central clump of papyrus — either for symmetry or perhaps in order to show both aspects of the body. The strip of water, with stylised ripples, is seen from above (see plate 8), yet the lotus flowers and birds on the surface and the fish in the depths are drawn upon it in profile, as are the two fish about to be speared, conceived, it seems, as sheltering in a small pool within the thicket. The painting is not quite finished, the papyrus and other details lacking the final outlines (see the enlargement), and the inscriptions also remain to be added.

The fragment, originally duplicated like the other — the spear of the second figure is visible at the base of the papyrus — is similar in format and in the conventions applied to the various elements of the composition. It is, however, completely finished, with all the outlines drawn and the inscriptions filled in, and is remarkable for the quality of the painting. The scaliness of the fish swimming among the lotus blooms, the delicate plumage of the different birds and the varied flight of the butterflies are amazingly natural, though none perhaps so striking as the detail of the furry hunting cat which leaps to pull down its quarry.

**Plate 24** *Banquet scene with musicians.* Painting on plaster. Height of musicians 10 in. (25.5 cm.). Mid eighteenth dynasty. From the tomb of Nebamūn at Thebes. British Museum, London.

Though their precise relationship is uncertain, these two fragments, together with a third, evidently formed part of a single scene representing a banquet, with entertainment provided by female musicians and dancing girls. The guests, dressed in the fashion of the years just before the Amarna 'revolution' (see plate 25), are seated in pairs in separate rows, the group of men being diversified by the alternation of full garment and wig with short kilt and cropped hair, and the ladies by the turning of two in the opposite direction (see plate 21). The principal interest lies, however, in the figures of the entertainers, grouped in the foreground, represented by the lowest register. Two of the musicians in one group are depicted almost full-face, which is rare, while the central element of the other is a lute-player posed in an unconventional yet characteristic manner (see figure 23 and plate 21). The treatment of the dancers, deftly outlined in true profile, is also unusually sensitive in the balanced opposition of the two figures and the suggestion of lively movement. The soles of the musicians' feet are shaded, an early instance of the technique (see plate 48), and the elaborate pleating of the ladies' robes is indicated in a somewhat similar way.

**Plate 25**  *Guests at a banquet*. Limestone, carved in low relief. About two-thirds life-size. Mid eighteenth dynasty. In the tomb of Ramose at Thebes.
The row of seated guests, relations of the vizier, from which this detail is taken (see plate 24) belongs to the earlier phase of the decoration of the tomb, executed in the polished manner of the era immediately preceding the Amarna interlude (see figure 20). The carving of the reliefs, particularly the modelling of the faces and the detail of the wigs and collars, is of the highest quality, the work having been abandoned before the final painting and only the eyes drawn in black outline.

**Plate 26**  *Head of a queen*. Yew wood, inlaid and painted. Height 4¼ in. (10.5 cm.). Mid eighteenth dynasty — Amarna period. From Gurob. Staatliche Museen, Berlin-Dahlem.
The head was originally part of a composite statuette (see figures 2 and 10), the body and crown (attached to the spike) having presumably been of other materials. Only one earring, of gold and lapis lazuli, is now visible through the layer of linen and gesso, once covered with blue beads, by which the headdress was altered in antiquity. The piece is generally assumed to be a portrait of queen Tiy, the mother of Akhenaten, but the identification is not certain and the features may in fact be those of her daughter Sitamūn.

**Plate 27**  *Akhenaten, Nefertiti and three of their daughters*. Limestone, carved in sunk relief and painted. Height 1 ft 5 in. (43.5 cm.). Amarna period. From Amarna. Egyptian Museum, Cairo.
Designed as a private altar, this small stela, in the exaggerated style of the early part of Akhenaten's reign, trespasses upon the private life of the royal family, an unconventional subject, but one repeated on other monuments of the Amarna period (see plate 30). The king and queen, informally posed, sit at ease with three of their daughters, the little group being knit together in various ways — by the union of the footstools, the attitude of the eldest child, the glances of the parents, and the extended rays of the sun disk, the Aten, offering the symbol of life. Though the effect is somewhat marred by the peeling paint, the actual carving of

the figures is quite careful, with hands and feet correctly represented and a certain elegance in the curving lines of the bodies, the streamers, and the modelling of the drapery (see plates 33, 34 and 35).

**Plates 28 and 29**  *Torso of a princess*. Quartzite. Height 6 in. (15.5 cm.). Amarna period. From Amarna. University College, London. *Torso of a queen or princess*. Quartzite. Height 11¾ in. (30 cm.). Amarna period. Possibly from Amarna. Musée du Louvre, Paris.
The Amarna concept of the ideal female form is perfectly exemplified in these two youthful bodies, the one entirely naked, the other lightly draped in a diaphanous robe through which the ripe contours are quite clearly visible. The interest in drapery as such, so very apparent in the treatment of the larger piece, is typical of the period, and had indeed considerable influence on later art (see figure 17 and plates 39, 40, 42 and 48). The smaller torso was originally part of a group and may have joined hands with another figure to the left, while in both cases the right arm was apparently extended forward, perhaps holding a fruit or flower (see figure 2), or, as in many Amarna reliefs, a sistrum rattle. Such freedom of gesture is extremely rare in stone statuary, and no sculpture with the arm held thus has survived intact, though other broken examples are known, as well as an unfinished piece with the bent arm merely blocked out. A metal pin in the shoulder of the Louvre statuette seems to indicate that the raised arm broke and was repaired in antiquity.

**Plate 30**  *Two of the daughters of Akhenaten*. Painting on plaster. Height of left figure 9 in. (23 cm.). Amarna period. From Amarna. Ashmolean Museum, Oxford.
Unusual in not coming from a tomb, the fragments (now reunited), of which this is the best known detail, were originally part of a palace mural showing a royal family group (see plate 27). The two little princesses have typically elongated skulls, full hips and thighs, and fragile legs in the Amarna manner, and the feet of both and the hands of one are correctly drawn (see figure 7 and plate 27), the eyes, however, following the usual convention. The poses, though deliberately balanced, are relaxed and natural, and the figures are closely linked by physical contact and mutual interest.

**Plate 31**  *Nefertiti making an offering*. Sandstone, carved in sunk relief, with traces of painting. Height 7¼ in. (18.5 cm.). Amarna period. From Amarna. Ashmolean Museum, Oxford.
The cutting of the figure, identified as Nefertiti by the characteristic blue crown (see plate 32), is remarkably neat for work in sandstone, though its quality will have been somewhat obscured by the painting, of which traces remain. The surface of the fragment is slightly

curved, indicating that originally it was part of a column.

**Plate 32** *Portrait head of Nefertiti*. Limestone and plaster, painted. Height 1 ft 7 in. (48 cm.). Amarna period. From Amarna. Staatliche Museen, Berlin-Dahlem.

Surely the most famous of all Egyptian pieces, the polychrome head of Nefertiti, found in the studio of Thutmose at Amarna, was evidently a sculptor's master portrait used as a model for other studies (see figure 11). The head is of limestone supplemented with plaster, fairly thick on the crown and shoulders, but on the finely modelled face and neck no more than a foundation for the pigment. Except for the eye sockets and the blank ends of the shoulders it is entirely painted, the crown and ornaments as they were in reality, the skin an unusually natural flesh tint, with the lips full red and the eyebrows and eyelashes outlined in black. The single eye — the other seems never to have been inserted — consists of a shell of rock crystal (the cornea) with a patch of black material, possibly wax, on the reverse to represent the iris and pupil, the white being simply the unpainted socket. Its charm enhanced by the delicate poise of the slender neck and the imaginative counterbalance of the headdress, the piece has all the grace of the Amarna period, but without the exaggerated mannerism of its earlier phase.

**Plates 33, 34 and 35** *Smenkhkarē and queen Meryetaten*. Limestone, carved in sunk relief and painted. Height 9½ in. (24 cm.). Amarna period. Possibly from Amarna. Staatliche Museen, Berlin-Dahlem. *Tutankhamūn and queen Ankhesenamūn*. Wood, gilded and inlaid with silver, glass and faience. About 1 ft 9 in. (53 cm.) square. Late eighteenth dynasty. From the tomb of Tutankhamūn at Thebes. Egyptian Museum, Cairo. *Tutankhamūn and queen Ankhesenamūn*. Ivory veneer on wood, carved in low relief and painted. Height 1 ft 0¼ in. (31 cm.). Late eighteenth dynasty. From the tomb of Tutankhamūn at Thebes. Egyptian Museum, Cairo.

Probably executed within a decade, these three pieces, the work of sculptor, jeweller and cabinet maker respectively, provide a striking illustration of the unity and consistency of Egyptian representational art, while at the same time documenting quite clearly the gradual return to orthodoxy during the reign of Tutankhamūn. The delicate little relief, perhaps intended as a mural plaque, is in the style of the later years of the Amarna period, with the contours of the body somewhat exaggerated, and the king languidly posed, his dress tricked out with dancing ribands. On the throne also, his successor lounges easily, but the outlines of the figures, particularly of the queen, are more restrained, and so too are the decorative streamers. On the box both king and queen are more formally represented, and without immediate intimacy, the streamers are almost stylised, and the influence of Amarna is chiefly felt in the sensitive treatment of the drapery and the gaiety of the garlanded pavilion.

The feet of the various figures are correctly drawn — even the curious poise of the king's left foot on the little plaque is adroitly managed — but the hands are rather less successful, the awkward position of the king's right hand on both plaque and throne having defied the draughtsman. Though the heads are in profile, the crowns of both figures on the throne and of the queen on the box are viewed from the front, and on the throne the floral collar resting upon the tall wreathed stand is seen in plan. In none of the representations is the flesh tints of the male and female figures differentiated.

**Plate 36** *Innermost coffin of Tutankhamūn*. Gold, inlaid with semi-precious stones and glass. Height 6 ft 1¾ in. (1 m. 87.5 cm.). Late eighteenth dynasty. From the tomb of Tutankhamūn at Thebes. Egyptian Museum, Cairo.

The solid gold coffin with its delicate cloisonné decoration and other adornments is an outstanding instance of the sheer technical expertise of the Egyptian jeweller and metalworker. The beaten gold, some 2.5 to 3.5 mm. in thickness, is finely polished and engraved, and the thousands of small inlay pieces are individually shaped to fit their frames. The face, the eyes of which were originally inlaid, is clearly conceived as a portrait and may be compared with other known representations of the king (see plate 37).

**Plate 37** *Colossal statue of Tutankhamūn*. Quartzite, partially painted. Height 9 ft 2 in. (2 m. 80 cm.). Late eighteenth dynasty. From Medinet Habu, Thebes. Egyptian Museum, Cairo.

This damaged colossus, of which only the head and torso survive, was one of a pair made for Tutankhamūn but inscribed and erected by his successor Ay and subsequently usurped by Horemheb. While the clothing, headdress and collar were painted, the flesh was represented by the natural red-brown of the stone, with only the eyes and lips picked out in colour (see plate 47).

**Plate 38** *Monumental lion of Tutankhamūn*. Granite. Length 7 ft 1 in. (2 m. 15 cm.). Late eighteenth dynasty. From Gebel Barkal. British Museum, London.

One of two lions intended for the temple of Soleb by Amenhotpe III, this, the second, was left unfinished in the quarries at Aswan. Some twenty years after, it was completed and inscribed by Tutankhamūn, and subsequently transported by his successor Ay — the removal of both lions to Gebel Barkal dating from a later period. Though the pose is natural and the treatment of the body comparatively realistic, the maned head, turned to face the viewer, is very stylised (see plate 19), and the piece remains in essence an architectural sculpture.

**Plate 39** *Statue of the wife of Nakhtmin.* Limestone. Height 2 ft 9½ in. (85 cm.). Late eighteenth dynasty. Egyptian Museum, Cairo.

Extraordinarily sophisticated in style and execution, the figure originally formed part of a dyad (see plate 6), now shattered, with the head only of the husband preserved. The lady's name is lost, but the man, Nakhtmin, was a military commander and court official under Tutankhamūn and possibly also under his successor, and the group may therefore be dated to the years immediately following the death of Akhenaten. The sensitive modelling of the ripe body beneath the drapery and of the drapery itself, the pleats lightly carved in relief, reflects the influence of Amarna sculpture (see figure 17 and plate 29), while the elaborate wig, minutely detailed, recalls the fashion of the period before the 'revolution' (see plates 24 and 25). The piece does not appear to have been coloured, though the eyes and eyebrows are outlined in black and the lips painted red, the absence of detail on the broad collar and the bands on the wig suggesting that these too may have been decorated, perhaps with gold leaf.

**Plate 40** *Amenmose and his wife Depet.* Limestone, carved in low relief and painted. Height 1 ft 10½ in. (57 cm.). Late eighteenth dynasty. Musée du Louvre, Paris.

The delicate carving of the relief and the details of dress, wigs and personal ornament show this fragment to belong to the latter part of the eighteenth dynasty (see plates 25 and 39). That it may be dated more closely to the period immediately following the Amarna interlude is suggested by the elaborate pleating of the linen garments (see figure 17 and plates 35 and 39) and the apparent assimilation of the man's facial cast to that of Smenkhkarē and Tutankhamūn (see plates 33, 34 and 35).

**Plate 41** *The goddess Isis.* Limestone, carved in low relief and painted. About life-size. Nineteenth dynasty. In the temple of Sety I at Abydos.

The very fine modelling of this detail is typical of the whole temple, though the colouring here and in the other small shrines is better preserved than elsewhere in the building. The figure of the goddess, painted the customary yellow (see plates 3 and 5), is conventionally represented — though with correct hands — her crown shown from the front (see plates 42 and 53) and the straps of her dress so disposed that they no longer cover the breasts as in reality. The whole scene is bordered and interspersed with inscriptions which identify

the figures and indicate the words which they speak.

**Plate 42** *Sety I and the goddess Hathor.* Limestone, carved in low relief and painted. Height 7 ft 5½ in. (2 m. 27 cm.). Nineteenth dynasty. From the tomb of Sety I at Thebes. Musée du Louvre, Paris.

Though the detail is a little obscured by the painting, the quality of this relief, from a pillar in the king's tomb, is comparable to that in the Abydos temple (see plate 41). The figures, named in the hieroglyphs above, are posed in a conventional embrace and formally represented, with the goddess' crown turned to the viewer (see plates 7 and 41) and the hands identical — though the king's feet are correctly paired. The body of the goddess is painted an unconventional red (see plate 48), while the king's flesh tint is made to show through the transparent garment, the pleats of which are lightly carved and indicated by stripes of thicker painting (see plate 48).

**Plate 43** *Statue of the lady Naia, wife of Thay.* Limestone. Height 2 ft 11½ in. (90 cm.). Nineteenth dynasty. From Sakkara. Egyptian Museum, Cairo.

The precise date of the group from which this detail comes is uncertain, though clearly it belongs to the late eighteenth or nineteenth dynasty. While the combination of large, elaborately tressed wig and simple linen garment may be paralleled in the years preceding the Amarna period (see plate 25), the soft fullness of the body and facial features and a certain heaviness about the limbs suggest that the piece belongs to the reign of Sety I.

**Plate 44** *Statue of a queen or princess.* Limestone, painted. Height 2 ft 4¾ in. (73 cm.). Nineteenth dynasty. From the Ramesseum at Thebes. Egyptian Museum, Cairo.

The minute detail of the wig, collar and other ornaments, adeptly carved and retaining some of their original colour, is underlined by the simple treatment of the body, seen as veiled in a plain shift relieved only by a rosette at the breast. The face is idealised in the royal mould, with traces of paint on the lips and eyelids, and the crown of cobras may once have been completed with sun disk, horns and feathers (see plate 34). The provenance of the piece indicates that the lady belonged to the court of Ramses II.

**Plate 45** *The weighing of the heart of the scribe Any.* Painting on papyrus. Height 1 ft 3 in. (38 cm.). Nineteenth dynasty. From Thebes. British Museum London.

The judgement of the scribe Any, depicted with his wife as though alive, is represented by the weighing of his heart against a feather, symbolic of truth, in the presence of a company of gods. The weighing, watched by the soul in the form of a human-headed hawk, is performed by Anubis and the result recorded by Thoth, whose ape also squats on the balance, while a hybrid creature of the imagination awaits to destroy the heart should it be light in the scales. The combination of writing and pictorial representation is here particularly intimate, the names of the gods and the words spoken by Thoth and the deceased being supplied in hieroglyphs, while the whole scene is itself in the nature of an illustration to the funerary text of which it forms part.

**Plate 46** *Statuette of a priest and scribe of the god Thoth.* Limestone. Height 1 ft 0½ in. (31.5 cm.). Nineteenth dynasty. From Ashmunein. Ashmolean Museum, Oxford.
The formal stance of the man, broken only by the raising of the left hand, is pleasantly relieved by the sympathetic and natural treatment of the ape of Thoth which he carries on his shoulders. The animal is at once symbolic of his priesthood, and of his status as scribe of the god, and may be paralleled from a few other statues of New Kingdom date.

**Plate 47** *Colossal statue of Ramses II.* Granite, with traces of pigment. Height 8 ft 10 in. (2 m. 70 cm.). Nineteenth dynasty. From the Ramesseum at Thebes. British Museum, London.
The natural division between layers of black and red granite — the red uncommonly fine grained and not unlike quartzite at first glance (see page 28) — has been carefully contrived to fall along the line of the shoulders so that, with the colouring of the headdress, beard, collar and other details, the contrast will have been restricted to the flesh surfaces of the body and face. The latter are polished, but the parts to be decorated are, with the exception of the collar, deliberately roughened and preserve traces of pigment which may be the remains either of painting (see plate 37) or of an ochreous foundation for gilding (see plate 50).

**Plate 48** *Queen Nofretiri worshipping.* Painting on modelled plaster. About life-size. Nineteenth dynasty. In the tomb of Nofretiri at Thebes.
The figure of the queen is delicately modelled in the plaster with which the wall is faced, and skilfully painted in a manner which gives it additional depth. The form of the upper arm, as well as part of the girdle, is made to show through the transparent sleeves, the pleating of which is suggested by stripes of thicker painting (see plate 42), while the flesh itself, tinted an unusual pink (see plate 42), is shaded (see plate 24). This shading is most noticeable on the face and neck, where it is quite subtle, but also occurs on the arms and hands — the latter incorrectly drafted. The queen's

facial features are neatly delineated, and the details of her gold collar, vulture headdress and feathered crown minutely drawn.

**Plate 49** *Statuette of queen Karomama.* Bronze, inlaid with gold, silver, electrum and copper. Height 1 ft 11¼ in. (59 cm.). Twenty-second dynasty. From Thebes. Musée du Louvre, Paris.
Though most of the damascening which originally covered the lower part of the dress, as well as the gilding of the face, arms and feet, is now lost, the surviving inlay of the broad collar and about the waist shows this to have been a most sophisticated example of Egyptian metal sculpture. The treatment of the head and the elaboration of dress and ornament recall Ramessid fashions (see plates 44 and 48), and the position of the arms and hands suggests that the queen may have held sistra or a floral offering (see plates 31 and 35).

**Plate 50** *Statuette of Osorkon III.* Limestone, with traces of pigment. Height 7 in. (18 cm.). Twenty-third dynasty. From the temple of Karnak at Thebes. Egyptian Museum, Cairo.
The king prostrates himself in a pose already known from the New Kingdom, but instead of the usual shrine he offers a sacred barque (now lost), the figure perhaps commemorating an actual donation ceremony in the temple of Karnak. The carving is delicate, and reminiscent of the best work of the earlier eighteenth dynasty (see plate 20), traces of ochreous material on the headdress and kilt indicating that these were originally gilded.

**Plate 51** *Statue of the goddess Taweret (Thoueris).* Schist. Height 3 ft 1¾ in. (96 cm.). Twenty-sixth dynasty. From the temple of Karnak at Thebes. Egyptian Museum, Cairo.
'Part brute, part woman, and part god', the hippopotamus cast in human mould here attains a certain dignity through the sculptor's sensitive interpretation of the traditional form and his polished handling of the material. The goddess' rôle as protectress of women in childbirth is symbolised by the two enlarged hieroglyphs she supports with her forepaws.

**Plate 52** *Statue of the goddess Isis with the god Osiris.* Schist. Height 2 ft 8 in. (81.5 cm.). Twenty-sixth dynasty. From the temple of Karnak at Thebes. British Museum, London.
In this group a common theme has been freshly formulated, with the figure of Osiris reduced in scale to produce a more aesthetically satisfying composition. The essentially triangular profile of the piece is empha-

sised by the strong line of the enfolding wings, their patterned surface contrasting with the soft, rounded contours of the bodies. The work is not wholly finished, the carving of the left wing remaining incomplete.

**Plate 53** *Statues of the goddess Isis and the god Osiris.* Schist. Height 2 ft 11½ in. (90 cm.) and 2 ft 9½ in. (85 cm.). Twenty-sixth dynasty. From Sakkara. Egyptian Museum, Cairo.

The cubic character of Egyptian sculpture in the round is here particularly apparent, accentuated indeed by the block form of the base and throne and the somewhat simplified treatment of the figures themselves. Though stylised and impersonal, the statues, which form a pair, are technically very accomplished, the smooth modelling and finish being well adapted to the quality of the stone.

**Plate 54** *Statue of a hawk.* Basalt. Height 1 ft 6¾ in. (47.5 cm.), excluding the base. Thirtieth dynasty. Musée du Louvre, Paris.

Although its clean lines are perhaps enhanced by the loss of the feet and tail and of the rather incongruous double crown, the purely formal treatment of this sculpture is none the less impressive, the bold sweeping shape of the body and its high polish standing in marked contrast to the more detailed, almost naturalistic, modelling of the head, with its arresting inlaid eyes. The piece has generally been ascribed to the twenty-sixth dynasty, but certain parallels suggest that it is of somewhat later date, belonging perhaps to the years immediately preceding the conquest of Alexander.

**Plate 55** *Statue of Irethoreru.* Breccia. Height 1 ft 2¼ in. (36 cm.). Thirtieth dynasty. Possibly from the temple of Karnak at Thebes. Oriental Institute, Chicago.

The formal posture of this kneeling figure is more common in the period of the twenty-fifth and twenty-sixth dynasties, but the unusual material and some details of the execution indicate that this is in fact an archaising work of the latter part of the thirtieth dynasty.

# THE COLOUR PLATES

2

4a

4b

6

7

12

13

14

17

20

21a

21b

22A

22B

24a

24b

30

31

34

35

38

40

41

43

44

49

50

51

53 a            53 b